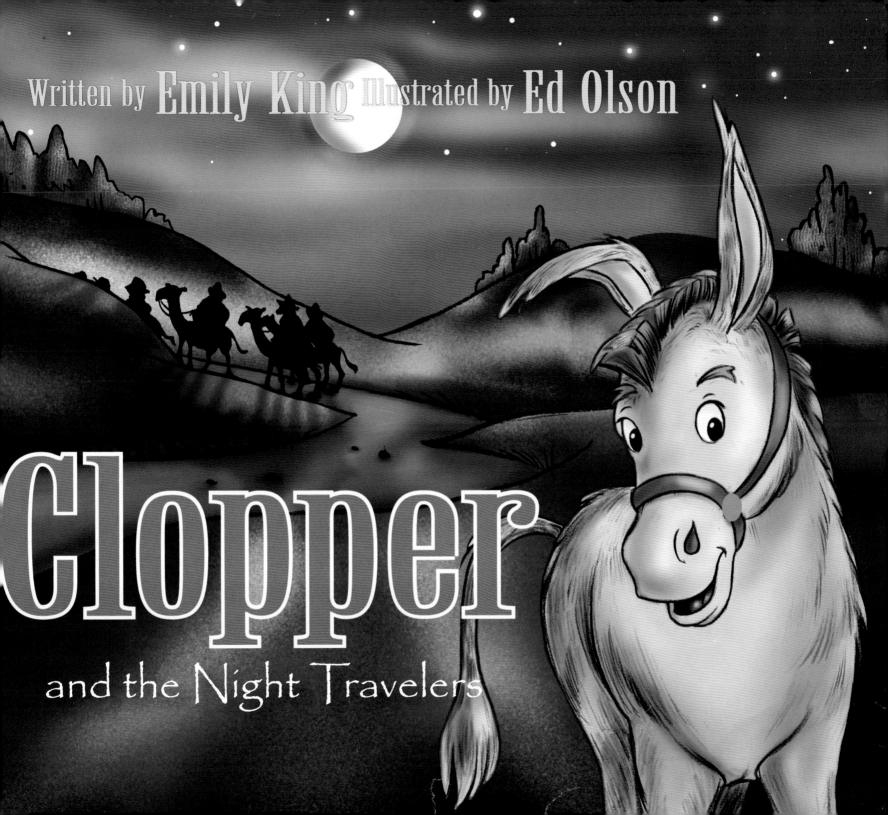

Written by **Emily King** Illustrated by **Ed Olson**

Clopper
and the Night Travelers

With love to
Jana, Caleb, Leslie,
Ryan, and Jamie.

May your life with Jesus
always be a wonderful adventure!

Clopper and the Night Travelers

Text © 2007 by Emily King
Art © 2007 by Ed Olson

Published by Kregel Publications, P.O. Box 2607, Grand Rapids, MI 49501.

ISBN 978-0-8254-3066-4

My name is Clopper. I was there when baby Jesus was born. What an exciting night!
But that was just the beginning of my adventures with Him. Listen, and I'll tell you more.

When the angels had left them and gone into heaven, the shepherds said to one another, "Let's go to Bethlehem and see this thing that has happened, which the Lord has told us about." So they hurried off and found Mary and Joseph, and the baby, who was lying in the manger.

Mary laid Jesus in the manger and the animals nestled down in the straw. Quiet settled over us. Before long, my sleepy eyes closed.

Suddenly, with a rustling and a bustling, three shepherds stumbled into the stable.

"We saw angels!" they said. "They told us the joyful news—Christ the Lord has been born!"
The shepherds saw the baby and fell to their knees. They were the first to come and worship
Jesus. But there were others who worshiped Him, too.

Simeon . . . praised God, saying: "Sovereign Lord, as you have promised . . . my eyes have seen your salvation." [Anna] gave thanks to God and spoke about the child to all who were looking forward to the redemption of Jerusalem.

Joseph and Mary took the baby to the temple in Jerusalem to dedicate Him to God. On the way home, they spoke about what had happened.

"Imagine—Simeon had a promise from God that he wouldn't die until he saw the Savior," Mary said.

Joseph smiled. "He blessed Jesus and called Him God's salvation. Then sweet old Anna said Jesus is the Redeemer that God promised long ago."

My ears tingled as I clip-clopped back to Bethlehem. I was carrying a very precious baby!

The star they had seen in the east went ahead of them until it stopped over the place where the child was. When they saw the star, they were overjoyed.

One evening, I snacked on new grass and gazed at the peaceful valley below. As the sky darkened, windows blinked with golden lantern light. Then a brighter light from a brilliant star beamed down on Mary and Joseph's house.

My ears stiffened. What was that? Thumping hooves . . . squeaking saddles . . . tinkling bells.

"The star!" a deep voice boomed. "It has stopped! Here!"

A party of strangers rode up the path. Camels snorted, stomped, and knelt, while foreigners dressed in elegant robes stepped down. One rider knocked on the door.

When Joseph saw the mysterious night travelers, he stuttered, "May . . . may I help you?"
The visitor bowed. "Good evening. We are magi—priests from the East." He pointed up at the sky. "We were led here by God, joyfully following this star. We traveled a long way to worship the newborn King."

The others bowed. "May we see Him?" the visitor asked.
Joseph nodded. "Please, come in."

On coming to the house, they saw the child with his mother Mary, and they bowed down and worshiped him. Then they opened their treasures and presented him with gifts of gold and of incense and of myrrh.

I peeked in the window. The magi gazed at Jesus and smiled. One approached quietly and set down a golden bottle.

"I offer this frankincense, sweet incense for the King," he said.

"This is myrrh," said the second one. "A costly fragrance for the King."
"Gold," said the third. "A precious gift to honor the King."
Then they bowed low to the floor and worshiped the baby Jesus.

Magi from the east came to Jerusalem and asked, "Where is the one who has been born king of the Jews? . . ." When King Herod heard this he was disturbed, and all Jerusalem with him.

When the wise men rose to leave, the tall one spoke to Joseph. "We went to Herod's palace in Jerusalem and asked where we might find the King of the Jews."

The older priest said, "We thought we would find all of Israel celebrating the King's birth. We were very surprised to find that no one knew about it."

The third one added, "Herod asked us to report to him when we found the child, so he might worship Him, too."

Joseph led them to the door. "We are honored by your visit. Please stay here and rest."

The magi's servants spread out tents and they all settled down for the night. The camels had already gone to sleep. I dozed off, too.

And having been warned in a dream not to go back to Herod, they returned to their country by another route.

About midnight, noises woke me. The wise men stood outside the tents and spoke in hushed voices.

"I had a dream," one said. "We are not to return to Herod to tell him where we found the child. We must go back to our country at once."

"I had the same dream," said another.

"Then we shall go. Quickly! Wake the servants."

Stirred from their sleep, the camels grunted and groaned. Servants loaded the supplies, then the magi mounted their camels.

The caravan set off down the path. Thumps, squeaks, and jingles faded into silence as the night travelers journeyed eastward in the moonlight.

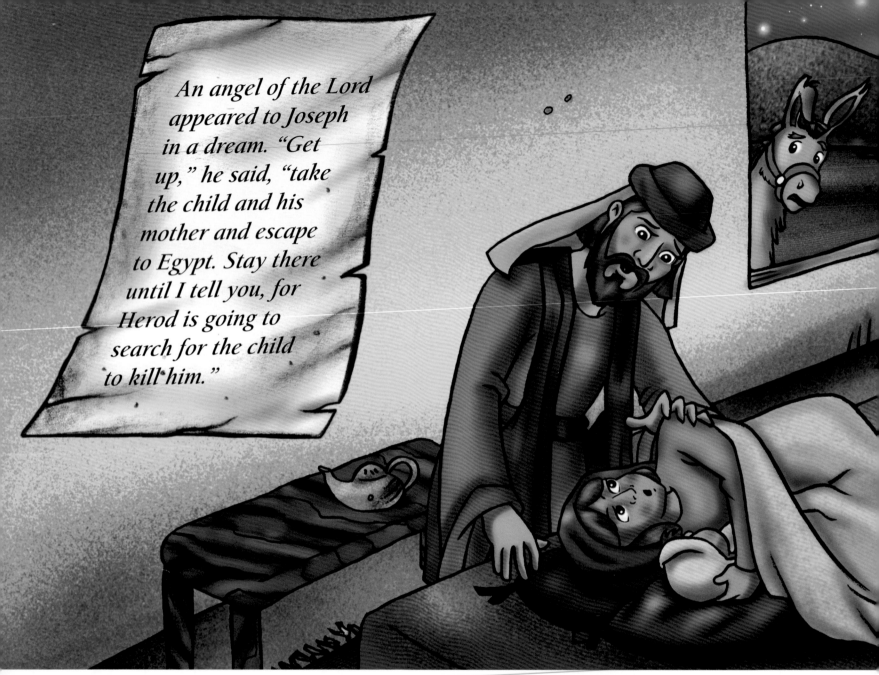

An angel of the Lord appeared to Joseph in a dream. "Get up," he said, "take the child and his mother and escape to Egypt. Stay there until I tell you, for Herod is going to search for the child to kill him."

I had barely drifted to sleep when I was awakened by Joseph's voice.

"Hurry, Mary," Joseph urged. "We must leave now."

Mary cuddled Jesus. "But it's the middle of the night," she whispered.

"I had a dream, Mary. An angel of the Lord told me to take you and the child and flee to Egypt. Herod is an evil ruler. He will look for Jesus, to destroy Him. We have to leave Bethlehem at once!"

The hair on my mane bristled. Jesus was in danger!

Mary and the baby settled on my back, then Joseph led us away. Now we were night travelers! In the moonlight, the rocks and trees cast long, dark shadows. I listened for Herod's galloping horsemen. But I heard only Joseph's heavy breathing, Mary's whispered prayers, and the clip-clop of my hooves on the stony trail.

"The Lord will protect us," Mary said. "Herod cannot hinder the plans of God."

In the morning, we stopped to rest beside a gurgling brook. I took a long drink, then munched on tender grass. Joseph spread a blanket for Mary and the baby and set out food.

Jesus cooed and smiled at His mother. She kissed His chubby fingers. "Joseph, how long until we reach Egypt?"

"Just a few days," he answered.

Mary stroked Jesus' cheek. "Soon we'll be safe in Egypt, my little one."

Joseph offered Mary some bread. "We never know where our path may lead," he said, "but we know that God leads the way."

Mary nodded. "When we follow Him, we know it's the right path."

Hee-haw! To me, that sounded like an adventure!

We finally arrived in the sun-baked land of Egypt. Merchants' carts overflowed with plump fruits and vegetables. I sniffed the air, spiced with cinnamon and cloves. Strange idols stood like towers above us. And there were camels . . . more camels . . . big smelly camels!

The people spoke a curious language, but Joseph found a man who could understand him.
"We need a place to stay," Joseph said.
The man told us to follow. We turned a corner and the man led us to a little stone house.
"Until God calls us back to Israel," Joseph said, "this will be our new home."

After Herod died, an angel of the Lord appeared in a dream to Joseph in Egypt and said, "Get up, take the child and his mother and go to the land of Israel, for those who were trying to take the child's life are dead."

One golden morning, Mary returned from the well with a bucket of water. Joseph stepped from the doorway and stretched, grinning from ear to ear.

"Mary, I've had another dream—a visit from an angel of the Lord."

"What did he say?" Mary asked.

"He said the evil ruler, Herod, is dead. Mary, we can go back to Israel now."

Mary dropped the bucket and hugged her husband. "Oh, Joseph. We can take Jesus and go home. Praise God!"

Hee-haw! We were going home!

When [Joseph] heard that Archelaus was reigning in Judea in place of his father Herod, he was afraid to go there. Having been warned in a dream, he withdrew to the district of Galilee, and he went and lived in a town called Nazareth.

When we got to Israel, Joseph heard that Herod's cruel son Archelaus ruled the land around Bethlehem. In a dream, God warned Joseph not to go back there. So we kept going north, all the way to Nazareth. That was a long trip and my hooves needed a rest!

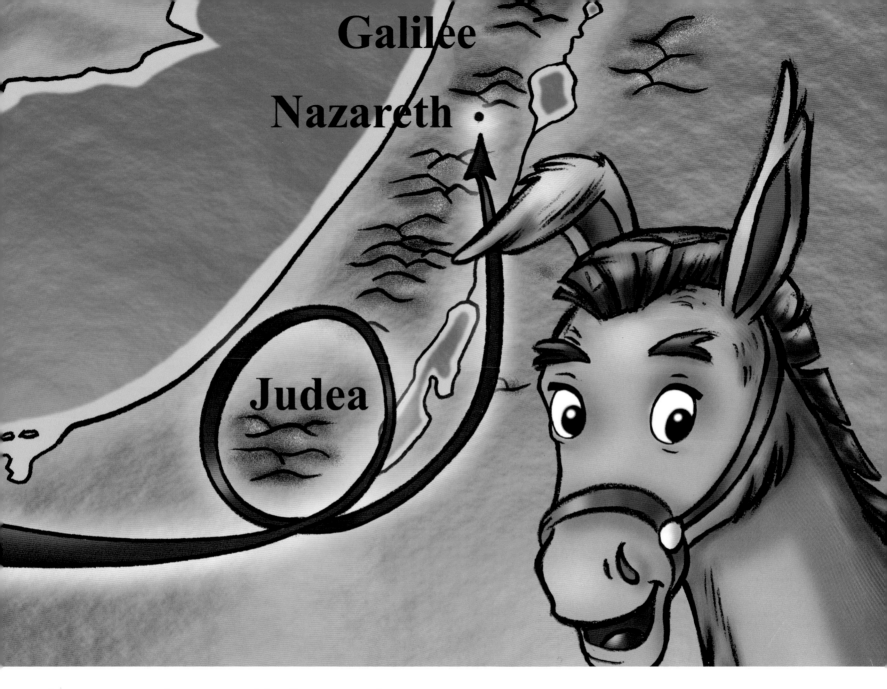

At last, we were home. God had protected His Son.

Jesus is God's only Son, the King above all kings and Savior of the world.
Some people understood how special Jesus is, like Simeon, Anna, the shepherds, and the magi.

I know how special Jesus is because I was there. And now you know, too!